Skateboarding:
Legendary Tricks
Steve Badillo
with Doug Werner

Tracks Publishing
San Diego, California

Photography by
Gavin Badillo
unless otherwise noted

Tricks performed by Steve Badillo
unless otherwise noted

Skateboarding: Legendary Tricks
by Steve Badillo with Doug Werner

Tracks Publishing
140 Brightwood Avenue
Chula Vista, CA 91910
619-476-7125
tracks@cox.net
www.startupsports.com

Copyright © 2007 by Doug Werner and Steve Badillo
10 9 8 7 6 5 4 3 2 1

The information contained in this book is based on material supplied to the Author and Tracks Publishing. While every effort has been made to ensure accuracy, and to attribute and credit all work, the Author and Tracks Publishing do not under any circumstances accept responsibility for any errors or omissions. Trademarked names are used in this book; however, instead of placing a trademark symbol beside every occurrence of a trademarked name, we state the trademarked names are used only in an editorial fashion and to the benefit of the trademark owner. No infringement of the trademark is intended. All images are owned by the Author or were obtained solely by the Author through private collections, or supplied courtesy of private collectors. With respect to the privacy of these individuals, all contributors and sources are credited with no association to possessions unless expressly requested otherwise.

Publisher's Cataloging-in-Publication

    Badillo, Steve.
       Skateboarding : legendary tricks / by Steve Badillo ;
    with Doug Werner ; photography by Becca Badillo, Gavin
    Badillo, Steve Badillo.
       p. cm.
       Includes bibliographical references and index.
       LCCN 2007908297
       ISBN-13: 978-1-884654-30-5
       ISBN-10: 1-884654-30-4

       1. Skateboarding. 2. Skateboarding--Pictorial works.
    I. Werner, Doug, 1950- II. Title.

    GV859.8.B335 2008   796.22
                           QBI07-600305

To
My daughter Sarah
And for my Ahma (In Loving Memory)
As one life begins another ends
May your ride be fulfilling

Acknowledgements

SkateLab
Todd Huber
Scott Radinsky
Gavin Badillo
Becca Badillo
Lance Mountain
Tony Alva
Steve Olson
Pat Ngoho
Paul Constantineau
Tom "Wally" Inouye
Kelly Lynn
Steve Steadham
Daewon Song
Richard Mulder
Nick Mclouth
Torey Pudwill
Tom Schaar
Matt Boyster
Chico Brenes
Peter Hewitt
Tony Hawk
Christian Hosoi
Sal Barbier
Danny Way
Jeff Grosso
Ed Hadvina
Jay Smiledge
DJ Farley
Mikey Pacheco
Mr. Pants
Bob-o Garza
Tim Trudell
Dorian Tucker
Frank Atwater
Phyllis Carter

Skateboard
Companies:
Powell Peralta
Santa Cruz
Alva Skateboards
IPS Skateboards
Dogtown
Vision
Sims
Tracker
G&S
Madrid
Hosoi Skateboards
H-Street
Santa Monica Airlines
Zorlac
Stereo
DC Shoes

Plan B
Steadham Skate Ind.
Flip
Gravity Skateboards
Black Label
Anti-Hero
Girl

Steve would like to thank
his sponsors for their con-
tinued support:

Alva Skateboards
SkateLab
DVS Shoe Company
Fury Trucks
Black Plague Wheels

Contents

What makes a Legendary Trick?

Is it the trick itself or the skateboarder who invented the trick? Maybe it's a group of skaters that is legendary or the area they come from. When I sat down to write my list of Legendary Tricks for this book, I quickly realized there are way too many to cover. So I narrowed it to the tricks and skaters that most influenced me and molded my skateboarding.

I tried to stay as true to the facts as possible. Research and investigation into these bits of skateboarding history often led to nothing more than a rumor. This meant that in a lot of cases I had to go straight to the source or other skaters from the period for details. These are the legends as I have heard them and grew up skating with.

Writing this book gave me the opportunity to meet and learn from some of the legends of skateboarding. In addition to being an instructional guide, it is my intention to open a unique window into skateboarding's past. I'm stoked to be able to share these stories and I hope they inspire skaters to learn some of my favorite Legendary Tricks.

— Steve Badillo

Part 1

Pioneers
Skateboarding enjoyed a revolution in the early 1970s with Improvements in skateboard design and wheel manufacturing. Before then, during the late '60s, steel and clay wheels with 2 x 4 planks of wood were considered skateboards. For years skateboards were toys found in the toy department and not thought of as marketable sporting equipment.

But soon innovative ideas from skaters and skateboard companies gave way for groups of skaters to start inventing legendary tricks. The Z-Boys from Dogtown, San Diego skaters, Nor Cal skaters and East Coast

skateboarders realized the potential for skateboarding to transform from sidewalk surfing to bank riding, pools, ramps and vertical transitions.

This was fertile terrain for early tricks to grow. Fundamental, creative and natural progression took root, and the first professional skaters legitimized skateboarding as a way of life and became legends. These pioneer skaters — sometimes individuals, sometimes more than one skating in different places at the same time — invented airs, grinds and lip tricks. Those tricks created the foundation for skateboarding to become not just another sport, but a lifestyle that would change the world. These are the skaters behind the tricks, and the tricks that advanced the sport and inspired the millions of skaters that would skate after them.

Photo credits
Lead photo of Tom "Wally" Inouye
Photographer: Steve Badillo

1 Bertslide

Bertslide

Born in Hawaii, Larry Bertlemann, aka "The Rubberman," was a prominent surfer and skateboarder during the late '60s and '70s.

> *How do you score a maneuver you have never seen before?*
> — The Rubberman

Larry invented the bertslide while skating and incorporated it into his surfing repertoire by laying his hand down onto the water while carving the waves. The bertslide can be done on banks, ramps, pools and flat ground resulting in a trick that can be performed anywhere by anyone. Larry said he surfed for himself and the public — not for the judges of contests. He was doing something totally new.

The Dogtown boys took his influential style of sliding and

> *The cutback (bert) was a very progressive move in surfing. To be able to change direction 180 degrees and slash off the white water and keep riding in the direction the wave was breaking was truly innovative.*
> — Tom "Wally" Inouye

adapted it to the banks, ditches and pools of Santa Monica and Venice. Jay Adams, Stacy Peralta, Tony Alva and the other Z-boys made the bertslide popular by adding variations to it like the 360 or 540 bertslides. Overrotating the slide gave it a stylish new depth.

Bertlemann had an unquenchable thirst for speed and riding on the edge. Years of surfing, skateboarding and motorcycles caught up with Larry in 1998. His adventurous lifestyle resulted in two degenerating disks, paralyzing the right side of his body. Luckily, surgery and therapy have restored his motion. The legendary bertslide is a fundamental trick for skateboarders to develop and learn board control.

Bertslide photo credits
Lead photo of Tony Alva, frontside bertslide
Photographer: Steve Badillo
Sequence of Steve Badillo, backside 540 bertslide
Photographer: Gavin Badillo

This is a backside 540 bertslide. Approach the bank with fast to medium speed — this helps with the rotation. Carve into the bertslide and put both hands down on the bank. Start sliding the board around 360 by pushing your tail foot backside.

Overrotate your slide for best results. As you come around the first 360, you may have to adjust your hands on the ground to help your board rotate.

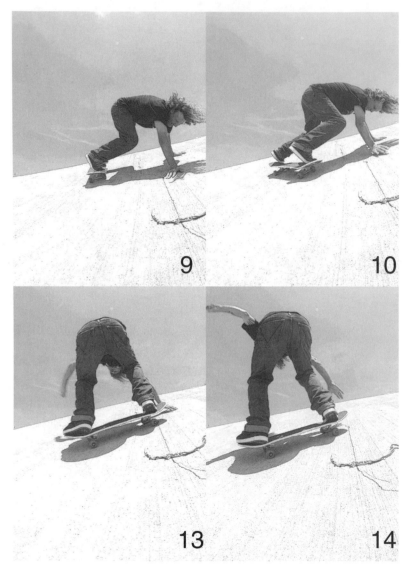

For the last 180, turn your head and shoulders around so your board can follow you. Push off the ground and swing the nose around leaning toward the flat bottom. Try it snakeskin style.

2 Wallride

Wallride

The wallride is a primal urge to attack a vertical wall with a kickturn. In the early '70s, when skateboarding started getting aggressive, young skaters would venture from bank to wall or flat ground to wall. Skaters like Bob Nichi were seen using little bank to walls to do backside kickturns around 1975 or 1976. I think the wallride is one of the tricks that skaters were able to perform at the same time in different places because of the new wheels and board designs of that day.

But the wallride stuck with one of the early pioneer skateboarders so much that his friends call him "Wally." In 1974 or '75 Tom "Wally" Inouye had a knack for doing the wallride before most other skaters, and he could do them high on the wall. Wally remembers skating Repetto Elementary School, which had a couple of banks and a downhill hallway. The school also had a wall about 3 feet high with only about 3 to 4 inches of bank at the bottom. Wally tried hitting the bank wall many times but didn't land it. Then one day when skating with his friends, Gary Zack, Jeff Walters, Dean Eddows, Jack Martin and Pat Driscroll, he attacked the wall at an angle instead of hitting it straight on.

This approach allowed Wally to land it almost every time. No one else could do it. Soon after his friend yelled out "Wally" and pointed to Tom. Tom's other friends joined in calling out "Wally." Since that day Tom was forever to be Wally. Wally became a notable pool rider in the '70s and launched his own company IPS (Inouye Pool Service).

Other skaters to do wallrides were Kevin "The Worm" Anderson, who did the Vermont drop in 1975. In 1977 Dave Hackett and Chris Strople did wallrides at Skatopia Skatepark, which had a brick wall coming out of the half-pipe. The trick gained further popularity when the skaters of Venice in the late '80s destroyed wallrides with variations and increased difficulty. Skaters like Aaron "Fingers" Murray, Jesse Martinez, John Thomas, Natas, Christian Hosoi and many others defined Venice skating with their wallrides.

I remember learning the wallride in San Fernando Valley at Balboa Banks. The banks were very wide. My friends and I would do a wallride, then a bottom turn and another wallride. We surfed Balboa Banks with wallrides all the way down the length of the banks.

All we tried to do is emulate an off-the-lip move from surfing.
— Tom "Wally" Inouye

With most wallrides you want to go as fast as you can. This bank to wall has a gap in it so I skated at an angle to ollie. Have your feet spread out as wide as you can for board control. Snap a little ollie and throw your weight up onto the wall. Let the board

suck up onto the vert by bending your knees and keeping your head in transition. Level the wallride out by keeping the board parallel with the ground. Now start to guide the board with your front foot by swinging it around 90 degrees.

As the nose comes around, your back foot should be putting pressure on the tail to lift the nose to get ready for landing. Compress and ride away. Now try frontside wallrides.

Wallride photo credits
Lead photo of Tom "Wally" Inouye, wallride
Sequence of Steve Badillo, wallride
Photographer: Jay Smiledge

3 Tailblock

Tailblock
The tailblock, aka tail tap, was a trick invented when skateboarders began skating pools and hitting the lip with speed. These guys would go up for grinds, grab the board and end up with the tail on the coping. This trick was made famous by skaters like Jay Adams, Tony Alva, Duane Peters, Steve Olson, Shogo Kubo and Paul Constantineau in 1976-'77. Paul Constantineau helped popularize it with his "Tail Tap" pro model from Dogtown Skateboards in 1978.

In the '70s, pool riding became the terrain of choice for pro skateboarders. The tailblock was a staple trick and variations started to emerge in magazines and ads. Frontside tailblocks, backside tailblocks, grabbing the nose with your backside hand, and grabbing the nose with your crail hand became

tricks worth notice. Pros like Peter Hewitt, Benji Galloway and Al Partanen do them today in pools, skateparks and ditches.

Tailblocks were also the name of the tail plate hardware that early skateboarders used to make the trick easier to balance on the tail. With different types of materials (wood, plastics and fiberglass) and styles of tailblocks, these skaters were able to attack the coping. Today's skaters are doing a greater variety of tricks that require a more streamlined board setup, so tailblock hardware has basically disappeared.

> *When riding in pools we did it a lot ... over at the Dogbowl. We would go up on top, pivot on the tail and drop back in ... going frontside and backside. Just surf skating.*
> — Paul Constantineau

Tailblock photo credits
Lead photo of Peter Hewitt, frontside tailblock
Photographer: Steve Badillo
Headshot of Paul Constantineau
Photographer: Steve Badillo
Sequence by Steve Badillo, frontside tailblock
Photographer: Becca Badillo

This is a frontside tailblock. This trick is best done on pool coping, parking blocks or cement blocks. Approach the top of the ramp with enough speed to stall on the coping. As you hit the parking block, reach down and grab the nose as your back wheels

hit the coping. Make sure your tail foot is on the tail
and secure. Roll up and stall your tail on the coping.
Your trucks and wheels should be in the air not
touching the coping. The only thing touching the
coping should be the tail.

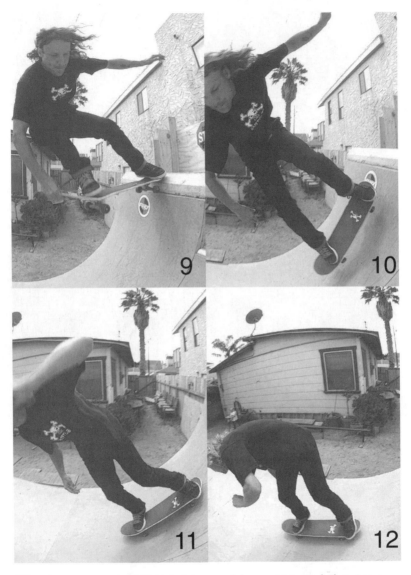

Pivot on your tail frontside and lean toward the transition. You may air back in the transition depending on the ramp. Roll away feeling stoked.

4 Frontside Air

Frontside Air

Tony Alva, aka "Maddog," is given credit for inventing the frontside air around 1977. The frontside air caused a turning point in skateboarding because the rider was able to leave the ground and blast vertically into the air. Although other skateboarders were doing it around the same time (San Diego skateboarders), Tony's style and ability to do it higher in pools made this trick famous.

Guys weren't doing airs on waves, guys weren't doing airs on snowboards ... we did the first airs on an extreme level ... not only to board sports, but first and foremost skateboarding.

— Tony Alva

Tony started and perfected the frontside air in the legendary Dogbowl and Gonzales bowl. The Dogtown boys practiced new moves with the assurance that they would not get kicked out or have the police coming around. This skateboard sanctuary provided the right environment for vertical tricks to be invented and perfected. Even with their different styles, guys like Jay Adams, Stacy Peralta, Paul Constantineau, Shogo Kubo, Jim Muir and others would push one another and feel free to progress skate-

boarding and find out what was possible. Carving with more and more speed, Tony discovered that he could smack the lip, bounce his back wheels off the coping, grab the board frontside with his indy hand in the tuck knee position, hang in the air and land it.

Every skater should have some form of frontside aerial trick. Whether it's indy, mute, lien, stalefish, tail grab or mellon, the air comes from the original frontside air tuck knee.

Frontside air photo credits
Lead photo of Tony Alva, frontside air
Photographer: DJ Farley
Sequence of Steve Badillo, frontside air
Photographer: Gavin Badillo

Frontside airs are fun and should be in everyone's bag of tricks. Skate as fast as you can. The faster you go, the higher the air will be. This trick can be done with an early or late grab, either way is fine. Hit the coping going frontside and snap your frontside

ollie. Grab the board with your indy hand directly in the middle of the board. Float as long as you can and start turning your nose back into the transition. As you land, try to hit the top of the transition to get good compression for the next trick.

8

9

10

11

5 Rock N Roll

> *The middle of the board can now be used as a focal point of making something happen on your skateboard in the world of tricks.*
>
> *– Steve Olson*

Rock N Roll
One of the first lip tricks most skaters learn is a rock n roll, especially when you are learning to skate transition. You start off with your fakies and kickturns, then your front trucks go past the coping and you do a rock to fakie. Now you're confident enough to combine kickturns and rock to fakie and it turns into a rock n roll. Now that you're ready to learn rock n roll, let's talk about where the trick originated.

In the late '70s, skaters with plenty of confidence created the rock n roll. As with many tricks, skaters invented maneuvers at the same time in different places. Legend has it that a skater in Northern California, Richie De Losada, was the first to do a rock n roll. Around the same time, Tim Marting from Alotaflex was given credit for the trick. But for all the skaters who were doing rock n rolls, one rider stood out among the others. In 1978 Steve Olson got the cover of *Skateboarder Magazine* doing a rock n roll. He won many contests with this go-to trick and combined it with lay back grinds. This took the trick to the next level with the boardslide rock n roll. Since then skaters have used the middle of the board to do tricks.

There are many variations of rock n rolls: frontside rock n roll, halfcab rock n roll, frontside lay back rock n roll, 360 rock n roll and others. But the traditional rock n roll in a backyard pool is still one of the coolest tricks.

Rock n roll photo credits
Lead photo of Steve Olson, rock n roll
Photographer: Steve Badillo
Sequence of Steve Badillo, rock n roll
Photographer: Gavin Badillo

This trick is done best on boulders. Have your feet spread out covering the front bolts and tail foot on the tail. You need only enough speed to get to the top of the ramp for this trick. Roll your front truck over the coping and put your wheels on the top deck

of the ramp. As you roll over the coping, start turning your head and shoulders back into the transition with your body a little twisted. The nose of your board will follow you if you turn your head and shoulders around enough.

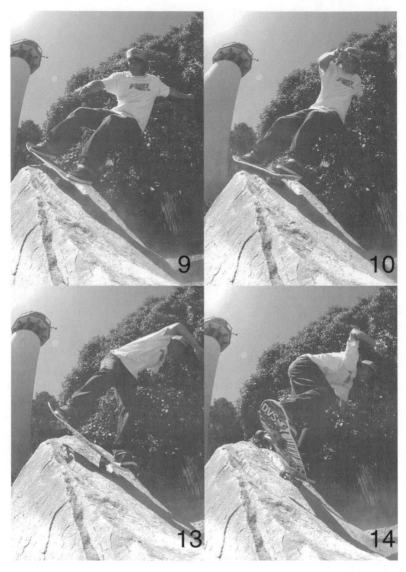

Then put some weight on the tail to lift up the nose and swing the board around 180 back into the transition. Compress and straighten out your knees. Now try a frontside rock n roll.

6 Millerflip

> *I saw him (Miller) do a Millerflip in the keyhole bowl at Lakewood working with Dale Smith, the coach of all coaches.*
> — Steve Olson

Millerflip

The first time I saw a pro do a millerflip was when I started skating cement parks. In the mid-'80s, there were not many near where I lived. I was too young to drive to parks like Upland Pipeline, Del Mar Skate Ranch and Skatercross. So when I could get someone to make the drive, I was stoked.

Skating up to the Combi Bowl in Upland is intimidating to a young skater. It's a big square bowl with a round bowl connected by a crazy shallow end that wasn't so shallow. I saw this kid skating the Combi with backside airs, lien airs and a frontside corner air in the square. Then I realized it was Steve Caballero. He made his lines look so easy — like anyone can do it. On his next run, he pulled out the millerflip in the round bowl. He went up and hit the lip, planted his hand frontside and pulled the board all the way around. It was so quick. I didn't even know what the trick was. The trick was named by the guy who invented it, Darrell Miller.

Around 1978, Darrell Miller was working on frontside inverts. He would just over-rotate the invert and slide into fakie. Miller was the resident pro at Skate City and had a reputation of being a gnarly skater. Jeff Grosso was a young skater at the time and recalls the intimidation Darrell Miller brought to the park, "Man he ripped." Miller had a moustache and would skate fast, doing stand-up grinds four blocks long. Then he would roll around, sit down and light up a Marlboro Red. Jeff remembers, "Whoa, he's smoking! Smoking is evil!"

When skating pool sessions, a lot of familiar tricks get thrown down, but this trick always gets cheers. Many pros like Duane Peters, Don Hamilton, Steve Caballero and Mike Vallely have performed this trick and have added many variations to it.

Millerflip photo credits
Sequence of Matt Boyster, millerflip
Photographer: Steve Badillo

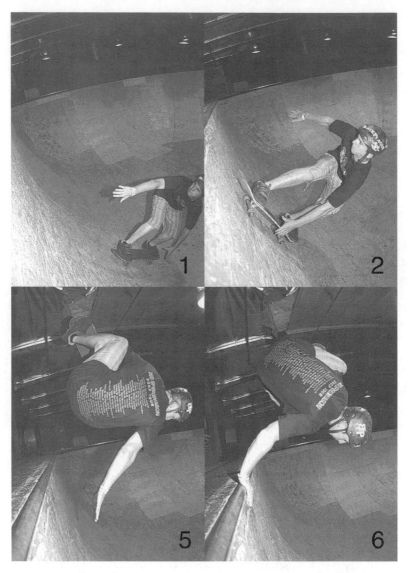

You need enough speed to spin all the way around, so medium to fast is best. Start by skating toward the coping and reach out with your indy hand reaching for the board. Grab indy and go into a frontside air, but you want to overrotate the board and body. Use

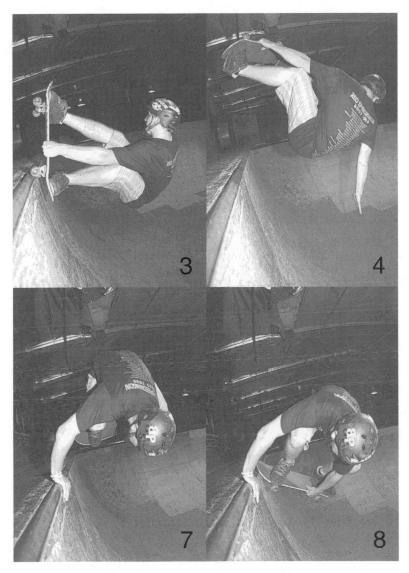

your backside hand to help the rotation. Now, with your backside hand, try to reach for the coping. You will be blind when you grab the coping, but the faster you rotate, the easier it will be to plant your hand.

As you come in, you want to ride away fakie so keep rotating and put the nose under the coping. Push off the coping with your planted hand and lean fakie. Compress and skate away.

7
Layback
Air

Layback Air

Florida's Kelly Lynn invented the layback air, aka layback invert. Kelly enjoyed doing frontside laybacks when surfing, so naturally he translated the trick to skateboarding. He started experimenting with them on banks at Moon Forest Skatepark in Ormond Beach, Florida in late 1977. Kelly began by doing frontside layback lipslides on banks. Then in early 1978, at a pool in Sensation Basin in Gainesville, he landed the layback air. The challenge became to get more upside down and to do them on bigger terrain. Before long he was doing them in the snake run at Sensation Basin, which had a true four feet of vert.

> *I remember going up with the intention of landing to tail and accidentally missing the edge of the pool on the way back in and almost making it. This caused a big light bulb to appear over my head and the very next one I tried to land inside the bowl on purpose and landed it first try ... it became my signature move.*
>
> — Kelly Lynn

Lynn became Florida's overall state champion at the age of 11 in 1976. He skated for Markel Skateboards while perfecting this trick. Other skaters like Mike McGill and Eddie Elguera popularized it on the West Coast. Some people thought Mike McGill had invented the layback air, but when questioned, he always gave credit to Kelly Lynn.

This trick is legendary because it was the first time skaters combined airs and inverts in pools and ramps.

Layback air photo credits
Lead photo and sequence of Kelly Lynn, layback air
Sequence of Steve Badillo, layback air
Photographer: Gavin Badillo

It's best to try it on a ramp that has some vert to it. Ride up to the lip with good speed. Make sure your feet are spread wide. Start reaching for the coping with your indy hand while you grab mute with the other. You should be grabbing your board and the

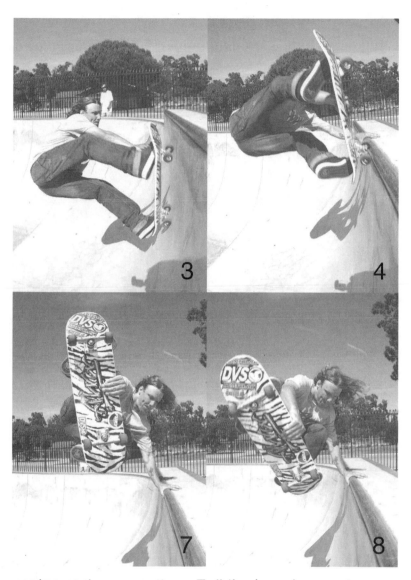

coping at the same time. Pull the board around
frontside like a frontside air, but put your weight on
your invert hand. Swing the nose around 180 and put
the board underneath your body.

Air back into the transition and let go of the coping. Compress and stand up for your rights.

8 Ollie

> *I never realized how many people were affected by one little move an eighty pound kid from Hollywood, Florida did in the Underbowl at Skateboarding USA way back in 1977.*
> — Alan Gelfand

Ollie

In the late '70s, vertical skateboarding was becoming popular and with it, vert tricks were being created. Around 1977 Alan Gelfand invented the ollie in Florida. Skateparks with more vertical walls were opening all around Florida. Ollie began by hitting the lip and popping little airs to lip-slides.

The next step was to pop no handed airs. Gelfand's friends had given him the nickname "Ollie." So when he was spotted pulling these aerials, the name and the trick were paired forever. Alan perfected the trick at skate-parks, halfpipes and pools. He used the ollie pop on vertical transitions. Stacy Peralta saw Alan do an ollie while on tour with Tom "Wally" Inouye and Greg Weaver in Florida in 1977. Gelfand became one of the first pro skaters for the newly formed Powell Peralta team in 1978.

Using the ollie, more and more tricks were being invented and realized by other skateboarders. Eventually Rodney Mullen popularized the flat ground version of the ollie, taking the trick from ramps and bowls to the street.

There are countless variations attributed to the ollie on all skateable terrains, including ollie-ing to grabs, flips, slides and stalls. The ollie is the fundamental skateboarding move for all skaters today.

Ollie photo credits
Lead photo of Steve Badillo, ollie
Photographer: Gavin Badillo
Sequence of Steve Badillo, ollie gap
Photographer: Gavin Badillo

This is the fundamental trick that affects almost all others. The better the ollie, the better the trick. This trick can be done on flat ground, banks or transitions. You will have better results if you are rolling before you snap. Place your front foot a little behind the

front bolts and your tail foot on the tip of the tail.
Bend your knees and jump up as you snap the tail to
the ground. Pull your front foot up toward the nose to
get lift and to level out the board.

Land with your feet covering the front bolts and your tail foot on the tail. For bigger ollies, snap the tail harder on the ground and keep practicing.

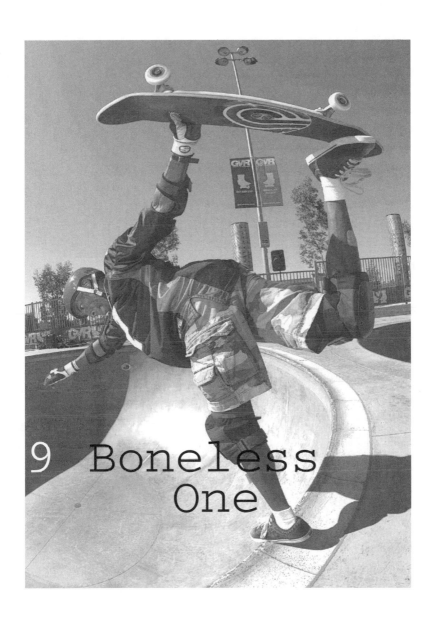

9 Boneless One

Boneless One
Gary Scott Davis, aka GSD, thought about the trick and didn't know if it was possible. First landed in Cincinnati during the early '80s, GSD and his friends refined the boneless by planting the front foot and blasting higher in the air. GSD first thought about using reverse movements of the foot plant. The name of the trick came from a child-hood puppet that one of his friends owned, called Harry the Boneless One. The boneless caught on in the 1980s because anyone could do it on almost any terrain. GSD was seen doing the boneless on the banks at the Del Mar Skate Ranch.

The boneless may have been invented on banks and small transitions, but when skaters started to

> *I learned the boneless one at Whittier. I did them on the hip at the Combi Pool in Upland. Back then, only a few skaters did them on vert ... one of the funnest tricks to do fo sho ... it is the coolest feeling.*
> — Steve Steadham

bring it to vertical ramps, many more versions helped define some skateboarder's styles and careers. Pros like Jeff Phillips, Steve Steadham, Monty Nolder and Buck Smith popularized the boneless one with many variations on vert ramps and pools. The boneless was the most popular way to get in the air until the flat ground ollie was invented by Rodney Mullen. The name was eventually shortened to boneless.

Aggrozone Hardcore Skate Shop held tryouts for their skate team near my home in the mid-'80s. I wanted to learn some tricks to do well in the tryouts, so my friend Mike showed me a bunch of boneless variations on the flat ground. With my new boneless variations along with street plants and boardslides, I made the team and got my first shop sponsor.

Boneless one photo credits
Lead photo of Steve Steadham, backside boneless
Photo: Ray Zimmerman
Sequence of Steve Badillo, frontside boneless
Photographer: Gavin Badillo

The boneless is a trick that can be done anywhere
— ramps, banks or flat ground. Ride up to the bank
with plenty of speed. Bend your knees and reach
down to grab indy. For the best extension, try to grab
between the middle to front truck area. Plant your

front foot down on the ground as you grab the board. Lift the board and turn frontside 180. Extend your tail foot out for a full boneless position.

Jump up from your planted foot. You will be in the air for a second. Bring your front foot back to the board while in the air. Let go of the board and lean into the transition. Land it compressed and straighten out. Now try it with a finger flip.

Part 2

Vert & freestyle's second wind

The vertical era started in the early 1980s with rising skateboard super-stars like Tony Hawk, Christian Hosoi, Lance Mountain, Mike McGill, Gator, Jeff Phillips, Neil Blender, Steve Caballero, Chris Miller and others. These guys took the fundamentals of the pioneers to vertical riding and used creativity to show the world that skateboarding had something to offer — something that young skateboarders could look up to, emulate and progress with.

The mid-'80s were filled with pro skaters inventing new tricks almost daily. Contests, demos and touring helped vertical skate-boarding become the dominant style. This was the golden age of vertical skateboarding.

During that same time, freestyle skate-boarding got a second wind with skaters like Rodney Mullen, Per Welinder, Kevin Harris, Primo Desiderio and others. Freestyle skate-boarding had its roots in the late '60s and early '70s, but faded when newer tricks, pool and ramp riding seemed to be the future of the sport.

Rodney Mullen led the way for freestyle's comeback with his dynamic style of skating. Rodney invented the most progressive tricks in freestyle, which eventually led to the street-style movement in the '80s and early '90s.

10 Lien Air

Lien Air

One of the most influential skateboarders of all time is Neil Blender. When skateboarding advanced with some artistic direction, Neil was at the forefront. He invented tricks as well as board graphics. Neil Blender is a legendary skater because he made the skateboard more than just a piece of wood to do tricks with. The board was transformed into an artistic creation that made kids want to buy them because of what he put on them, not just what he did on them. Neil Blender's skateboards are now some of the most coveted and valuable decks in skateboarding.

In the late '70s Neil invented the lien air. Basically, he took his name and spelled it backward to name the trick. It works out well because when you do this trick, you actually have to lean into it to make it work. This trick was quickly adopted by pros like Steve Caballero, Tony Hawk, Lance Mountain and others.

Ramp of the Gods was the name of my friend's backyard vertical ramp where I learned to do airs. My friend Daniel could do lien airs, and I wanted him to show me how to land them. He said, "This trick is frontside, and you air in blind on the landing. You should stay on top of the air and lean over your front foot." On his ramp doing an air at the coping or above it was an accomplishment. Once I had them down at the coping level, Daniel and I competed to see who could do them the highest. His airs were almost always higher than mine, but once I dropped in and did a backside air for more speed and went into a lien air and popped out higher than usual.

I held the board too long and thought I could bring the wheels back in. Smack! I hung up on the coping going face and shoulders first into the transition. I thought I lost my front teeth, but I only had blood in my mouth. I didn't do lien airs for a few months after that, but the intimidation didn't last. I love lien airs and continue to do them.

Lien air photo credits
Sequence of Steve Badillo, lien air
Photographer: Gavin Badillo

Lien airs are normally done on ramps, pools or hips. Skate up to the coping with plenty of speed. Ollie or float your air frontside, grabbing either right behind your front foot or the nose of your board.

3   4

7   8

Pull your front foot toward the nose to get more air. Lean frontside and rotate the nose 180 and land just under the coping. Let go of the board and compress. Nice. Now go listen to Neil Blender's band.

I saw Brad Bowmen wearing a T-shirt of himself doing a backside air but tilted frontside to what we called a lien air in 1980 at the World Cup Series. Then I saw Eddie "El Gato" Elguera do that trick in the contest and convinced myself that he was inspired by that same shirt.

—Pat Ngoho

9

10

11

11 Sad Plant

Sad Plant

One of my favorite skaters of all time is
Lance Mountain. He has witnessed skateboarding evolve and progress through the
years and has influenced the sport in a posi-
tive way. In 1980 he was skating a skatepark
in Anaheim,
California called
Sadlands or
Moon Park. It
was a dual play
on names
because of the

> *If it is done right it looks
> good. Only a few people
> did them good and the
> name is catchy.*
> — Lance Mountain

moonlike crater sculptures that were skateable, but sad because of how small they
were. Lance was doing inverts on the sculptures and was pointing the nose out to help
stall them. Neil Blender shot a photo of Lance
doing this unique trick. Looking at the photo
later, he named that method of doing an
invert a sad plant.

When done right, the trick looks stylish and
cool. The sad plant received a lot of coverage
in skate magazines and in ads. Several years
later when the video, *Search for Animal Chin,*
came out, the sad plant reached many more
skaters and became very popular. Lance is
still asked by skaters to bust out his leg-

endary sad plant.

The sad plant is one of those inverts that has style. Skating in the late '80s, street skaters took the sad plant vert trick to the flat ground and started doing street plants. We all did a lot of street plants like ho-hos, one-footed plants, fingerflip variel plants, wallride to street plants, yo-yos, street sad plants and many more.

But then street plants died out. I tried to do them on ramps but mine were sad. So I didn't do them for years until I was hired by Ashley Simpson for one of her print ads. I did the sad plant for the ad and Ashley liked it.

Sad plant photo credits
Lead photo of Lance Mountain, sad plant
Photographer: Steve Badillo
Sequence of Lance Mountain, sad plant
Photographer: Steve Badillo

You should learn to do normal inverts before trying the sad plant. Skate up to the coping with enough speed to do an invert, about medium speed. When you almost hit the coping, start reaching for the board with your mute hand, and at the same time

with your other hand, start reaching for the coping.
Grab the board and the coping and let your body get
inverted.

Go into the traditional invert position and while stalling on your invert hand, point your front foot out to go into the sad position. Once in the sad position you will start to fall back into the transition. Keep looking into the transition as you re-enter.

Let go of the coping and air back in. Compress and stand up. Classic.

12 Nosepick

Nosepick

Some tricks are invented by many skaters at the same time and some tricks have no one claiming credit. The nosepick first appeared in the mid-'80s with pros like Tommy Guerrero, Ben Schroeder and Mike Vallely. I think it may have started on vert ramps with pros like Danny Way, but when mini ramps started to get popular nosepick variations exploded on lip trick ramps.

Check out any skate video of the era and you'll see all sorts of dudes picking their nose. These skaters made it a cool trick to do along with many different variations. Then, when street skating became popular, the nosepick was done in ditches, curbs and extensions. In any case, the nosepick continues to appear in videos and magazine ads showing that this trick is legendary.

A coper is a piece of hardware that goes over your trucks to make grinding easier. The downside is that if you slide out of a nosepick, you'll get a shinner. When I finally stopped putting copers on my Tracker Trucks, which was the truck of choice for me as a young skater, I learned nosepicks on high curbs. It was easier to frontside ollie nosepick stall on bigger curbs, grab the board and pull it back to the ground.

In Animal Chin, *Tommy Guerrero said never do a nosepicker with a coper.*
— Lance Mountain

Nosepick photo credits
Sequence of Steve Badillo, nosepick
Photographer: Gavin Badillo

Skate fast enough to get to the coping. Bend your knees, reach down and grab the board with your indy hand. Carve up to the lip at a slight angle. When your wheels almost get to the coping, pull up and do a little indy air. Then point your front foot onto the

coping and lift your tail up to pick the coping. It's sort of like a boned out nose grind, but grabbing with your indy hand. Stall for a split second and pull the board around leaning back into the transition.

Compress, stand up and roll away. Check for blood when doing a nosepick.

13
Smith
Grind

Smith Grind
The smith grind is considered to be one of the more difficult grind tricks. Evolving from the frontside grind, you point your front foot and lay your board on the coping while grinding. Some pro skateboarders

> The trick is sick ... the smith grind was taking the frontside grind to the next level. It even makes the skater develop style because of the body positioning.
> — Steve Steadham

were doing smith grinds without knowing it or would overgrind their stand-up frontside grinds while slashing the coping.

But in 1981 Mike Smith had refined the trick and gave it his name. In the '70s and '80s, when tricks were being invented every day, it was common for pro skaters to name tricks after themselves. Using this trick as a staple in his contest runs, he popularized it, especially at the '80s Gold Cup Series where Mike placed very well.

The smith grind is one of those tricks almost every skater learns to do because it can be done on most terrains. It can be performed with many variations on rails, ledges, ramps,

ditches, pools and curbs. The smith grind is so stylish it has defined some careers including those of Christian Hosoi, Dave Hackett, Mike Smith, Claus Grabke, Salba, Monte Nolder, El Gato and others.

The smith grind now is used as a combination trick were you combo into or combo out it. Examples are kickflip smith grind, lipslide to smith, smith revert, smith grind 270 out ... the list goes on and on. The potential for combos with the smith grind are endless.

Smith grind photo credits
Sequence of Steve Badillo, smith grind to fakie
Photographer: Gavin Badillo

The smith grind can be done on almost on any terrain — ramps, rails, ledges, pools and curbs. Approach the lip with speed. The faster you go, the longer the grind. Ride up the transition carving frontside. Lift the nose slightly and go into a frontside

grind. When the nose clears the coping, point your front foot under the lip. The board should be touching the coping with the front truck below the coping. Make sure your front leg is pointing under the lip with your knee straight. Hold the smith grind as long as

you can. In this sequence, I fakie over a spine. Just put your weight on your back foot and lean fakie. Lift the nose up a little to clear the spine as you roll backward. Turn your head and lean fakie. Stand up and skate into a fakie smith stall.

14 Christ Air

Christ Air
Holmes, aka Christian Hosoi, was the high-flying, big air, one-man skate-board show during the 1980s. Christian became one of skateboarding's favorite skaters. His style and presence was what skate-boarding needed — a personality.

He grew up skating skateparks like Skateboard World in Torrance, California. Around 1977, his father, Ivan Hosoi, began operating Marina Del Rey Skatepark, and Christian became the ultimate skate rat, skating every day and progressing uncommonly fast for a young skater. Even before he was old enough to drive a car, he invented the Christ air. Of the many tricks he invented, the Christ air is Hosoi's most famous. It is his signature trick.

Christian's fashion sense also took root in the skateboard culture. He started many trends  both on and off his board. Many pro skaters adopted the Christ air as a go-to trick, like Steve Caballero, Rob Roskopp and Omar Hassan. But none did it as high or with as much style as Christian.

The irony of the Christ air is that Hosoi invented this trick before he became involved with Christianity. After a drug conviction, Christian turned to Jesus and today he is active in both skateboarding and Christianity. Years later when asked about finding Christ he said, "From that moment, even though I was in prison, it was like I was the freest man in the world." (Christian Hosoi, *Secrets of Success*).

Christ air photo credits
Photo of Christian Hosoi
Photographer: Steve Badillo
Sequence of Steve Badillo, christ air
Photographer: Becca Badillo

Christ Air

I learned this trick in the '80s off of launch ramps, so
this is the launched Christ air version. Push off going
as fast as you can. I used a snake run to get speed.
Aim for the coping, bend your knees slightly and ollie
or launch out of the bowl. Reach down with your

backside hand and let the board come up into your hand. Take your feet off the board and lift the board up with both arms stretched out horizontally. Kick your feet down and pose in the Christ position. Hold it. Lean forward, start to put the board under your

feet and try to land with your feet on the bolts. Bend your knees and compress.

15
Rocket
Air

Rocket Air

Another one of Christian Hosoi's trick inventions is the rocket air. Growing up in Marina Del Rey Skatepark, which was also his first shop sponsor, he was free to skate all day long. He improved his style, going faster and higher every day. At one point Christian held the highest air record. In the early '80s, Hosoi gained superstar status after inventing the rocket air. He went on to form his own skateboard company, Hosoi Skateboards, one of the pioneers in skater-owned companies.

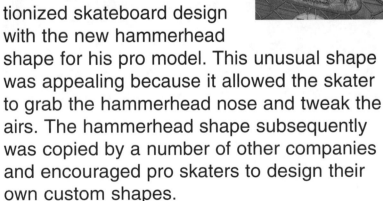

Hosoi Skateboards revolutionized skateboard design with the new hammerhead shape for his pro model. This unusual shape was appealing because it allowed the skater to grab the hammerhead nose and tweak the airs. The hammerhead shape subsequently was copied by a number of other companies and encouraged pro skaters to design their own custom shapes.

The rocket air is one of the vertical tricks that is still done by many of today's professional skaters. Danny Way recently did a backflip rocket air on the megaramp at the X-Games.

I had the unique experience of seeing Tony Hawk pull a ripping rocket air in tribute to Hosoi during the Legends of Vert demonstration at the 2007 Summer X-Games. Tony and Christian are in the photo above.

Rocket air photo credits
Lead photo of Tony Hawk, rocket air
Photographer: Steve Badillo
Sequence of Steve Badillo, rocket air
Photographer: Becca Badillo

Skate up the transition with a lot of speed. Launch and grab the nose of the board with both hands. Pull down your front foot to the tail of the board and straighten your legs into the rocket air. As you start to land, lift your front foot back to the front bolts.

Let go of the board and push your front foot forward to level out. Land, bend your knees and compress.

8

9

10

11

16 Madonna

Madonna

Tony Hawk, aka Birdman, has invented many, many tricks. His journey through skateboarding is really amazing. The madonna is one of his most famous tricks. In 1984, when combining a one-footed lien air and a lien to tail, the madonna was conceived.

Hanging out with Lester Kasai, Hawk asked why no one seemed to be doing his tricks. Lester replied that Tony should give his next trick a trendy name. Madonna was a popular singer at that time. Thus Tony used her name for the trick. Interestingly, the backside way of doing the madonna is called Sean Penn. Many pros still do the madonna, including Sandro Dias who is a top ranked professional vertical skateboarder.

Lester replied that he should give his next trick a trendy name. Madonna was a poplar singer at that time. Thus Tony used her name for the trick.

Madonna photo credits
Lead photo of Tony Hawk, madonna
Photographer: DJ Farley
Sequence of Steve Badillo, madonna
Photographer: Mr. Pants

Skate up the transition with enough speed to blast a frontside air. As you ride up the tranny, start reaching for the nose. Pop off the coping with your back wheels and grab the nose. At the same time take your front foot off the board and kick your leg down

into a frigid position with full extension. Lean frontside and aim the tail to smack the lip. Land on the tail and bring your front foot back to the bolts of the board. Lean back into the transition, compress and stand up.

Madonna

17 Airwalk

Airwalk

During the mid-'80s Tony Hawk seemed to invent skateboard tricks daily. One day in 1983 Tony Hawk invented the airwalk, and it became one of the most famous skateboarding tricks of all time. While Micke Alba was attempting one-footed judo airs, Tony took that trick further by taking both feet off the board — kicking his front foot out judo and his back foot out in the other direction.

Tony didn't have a name for the trick until he shot a sequence for *Thrasher*. When that sequence was published, the caption called it an airwalk. The name stuck and the shoe company "Airwalk" was born a year later. Other pros with notable airwalks are Danny Way, Christian Hosoi and Kevin Staab. A couple of years after Hawk performed the feat, Rodney Mullen took the airwalk to the flat ground and the ollie airwalk was born, combining vert and street.

Airwalk photo credits
Headshot of Tony Hawk
Photographer: Steve Badillo
Sequence of Steve Badillo, airwalk
Photographer: Gavin Badillo

Ride up the transition with enough speed to blast. As you hit the lip, start reaching down to grab the nose with your backside hand. Let your feet go off the board and kick your front foot out into a judo position, while your back foot moves into a frigit position.

When you start to land, bring both feet back to the board and on top of the bolts. Lean with the board and stand up. Now go try airwalking.

18 Japan Air

Japan Air

Every skater gets inspiration from other skaters and styles, even when you are a legendary skater like Tony Hawk. In 1985, after seeing a photo of a kid doing a tuck knee mute air in Japan, Tony along with friend Lester Kasai worked on refining the Japan air. Tony did this trick at Del Mar Skate Ranch. People freaked on how he completely tweaked out this mute grab air.

When street skating became popular, Japan airs could be seen everywhere. Pros like Tommy Guerrero, Natas Kaupas, Jesse Martinez, Mark Gonzales and many others took the Japan to launch ramps. The Japan grab became very popular at many street contests and demos of the late '80s and '90s.

People freaked on how he completely tweaked out this mute grab air.

This trick is great because if you get enough air, you can hold the Japan position and make it look so styly. You can also add variations including the Japan backside 180 or Japan one foot. I have enjoyed performing this trick since I learned it on launch ramps in my front yard.

Japan Air photo credits
Sequence of Steve Badillo
Photographer: Becca Badillo

Once again, speed is the name of the game. Approach the coping and pop off with your back wheels as you ollie. Grab the board with your backside hand but in the mute position just behind your front foot. With you're grabbing mute, start tweaking

the board into the Japan position by turning the nose 90 degrees frontside and lay down your front knee on the board toward the tail. When you start to land bring the nose around back 90 degrees to original mute air.

Lean forward and get centered, let go of the board. When your wheels hit the ground, compress and skate away. *Domo origato!*

Part 3

Streetstyle

With the vert era dying out, new professional skateboarders took freestyle and vertical tricks to the streets. In the late 1980s and early 1990s streetstyle had taken over the skate industry with new talent, style and marketability. Legends like Mark Gonzales, Tommy Guerrero, Mike Vallely, Jason Lee, Mike Carroll, Eric Dressen, Julian Stranger, Eric Koston and others changed the landscape of skateboarding with an urban, raw sense of style that millions of kids would soon relate to. When Rodney Mullen took the ollie from the vertical plane and mastered it on the horizontal plane, he laid the groundwork for street skating. This pushed skateboarding to a faster, longer and further level of progression than ever before. The streets became the terrain for skateboarders to envision the vast options and obstacles they would need to craft the art form of skateboarding. Combining vert, street and freestyle skating and being able to adapt to any terrain is the essence of being a well-rounded skateboarder.

19 Salad Grind

Chapter 19

Salad Grind

Eric Dressen, the street ripper kid with Venice roots, helped bring street skating to the forefront of the skateboarding industry. In 1988, with a raw, urban, aggressive style, Eric would have a trick to call his own. Skating in Vancouver, Canada at Kevin Harris Skate Ranch with John Lucero and Jeff Grosso, Eric Dressen was tweaking out his backside 5-0 grinds to slow down his runs. He really liked the way it looked so finally he tried it frontside.

The salad grind is very stylish and can be done on any lip, rail or ledge. I have skated with Eric Dressen many times and even though he is an influential street skater, it should be known that he invented this trick on a ramp. But Eric can skate it all — ramps, street, pools, ditches and more — and make it look easy. The salad grind is still one of his favorite tricks. Eric, in my opinion, is one of the great original street skaters.

But it wasn't until I took it back to San Francisco and skated with Tommy Guerrero and Kevin Thatcher that it became my namesake. Kevin Thatcher actually named it.
— Eric Dressen
Skateamerica.com

With your feet spread out over your board, skate up the ramp going fast so your grind can develop and be long. Go into a frontside 5-0 grind. Stand up on top of the grind and start to turn the nose toward the deck of the ramp.

Put your weight more on the back trucks to swivel the nose backside. Grind and hold it. Then turn the nose back into the transition and lean into it. Would you like any Dressen with your salad?

Salad Grind

9

10

Salad grind photo credits
Lead photo of Steve Badillo, salad grind
Photographer: Mikey Pacheco
Sequence of Steve Badillo, salad grind
Photographer: Mikey Pacheco

11

12

13

20 Ollie Impossible

Ollie Impossible

Legend has it that a freestyler said that it was "impossible" to flip the board around your foot, having the board actually rotate end over end, opposite of a kickflip. The legendary skater Rodney Mullen invented the ollie impossible in 1982, but didn't really perform it in contests until the mid-'80s. At the Skateboarding Expo in Canada around 1986, Rodney competed against the best freestylers in the

I learned them in 1990 when they were getting hot, almost a must-have to enter contests ... Rodney Mullen = Legend
—Daewon Song

world. There he pulled out his best combinations of freestyle tricks including the ollie impossible. When the judges announced their scores, Rodney received his first perfect 100, winning the world championship.

This trick is very difficult, but other pro freestylers learned the trick and adapted it to their routines. In the mid-'80s the vert era caused the trick to fade, but in the late '80s and early '90s street pro skaters like Ed Templeton and Jason Lee adopted the ollie impossible into their own style.

In more recent years the ollie impossible has made another return with pro skaters like Mathias Ringstrom doing them on the vert ramps. This trick has translated through three distinctive skating styles — freestyle, street-style and vertical skating — making it a legendary trick.

Ollie impossible photo credits
Sequence of Steve Badillo, ollie impossible
Photographer: Gavin Badillo

Try riding at medium speed. Make sure your feet are in ollie impossible position. Have your front foot near the front bolts, but with your heel hanging off the board. Your back foot should be on the tail with your toes scooping the edge of the board.

Bend your knees and snap the ollie. With your tail foot, scoop the board as it rotates 360 degrees around your tail foot. Bend your knees in the air and land your front foot on the bolts. Stand up then try to do a lawnmower.

21 Kickflip

Kickflip

The freestyle grand master and streetstyle godfather is Rodney Mullen. Among the long list of tricks that he invented, the kickflip is probably the most fundamental for street skating. This story actually starts back with the original freestylers of the 1970s. Guys like Kurt "Mr. Kickflip" Lindgren, Ty Page, Russ Howell and others did a freestyle kickflip. They found that a board could be flipped, not with an ollie, but with foot placement and their toes. There were many variations of this old-school kickflip.

This paved the way for Rodney to take it further when he invented the ollie kickflip in 1983. It was originally called the magic flip because nobody could figure out how Rodney did it. At first, it was a failed attempt at the ollie, but then he figured out that he could drag his front foot off the board and make it flip. Mullen perfected it and added variations to what became the ollie kickflip.

Gonz and Natas then took Rodney's stationary kickflip and translated it to the streets. They did kickflips off curbs and over small gaps. The trick became the staple of street tricks. When I first saw skaters like Gonz and Natas do the kickflip in videos, I was stunned how fast they were going. All my skater friends and I had to learn the kickflip. At first it was so awkward, flipping those big, wide boards of the '80s. I sprained my ankle once flipping my heavy tank board. As boards became more symmetrical and streamlined, kickflips became a lot easier to do.

A kickflip is the definition of fun to me … it opened the door for skate-boarding and made it what it is now.
— Torey Pudwill

Kickflips can be done anywhere and on anything. Start with your back foot on the tip of the tail and your front foot just below the front bolts. Make sure your front foot is at a slight angle with your heel hanging off the board. At any speed, bend your

knees to snap an ollie. When you start to ollie, pull your front foot up toward the nose and flick the board causing it to flip around. Keep your knees bent and up in the air so the board can rotate underneath you.

9

10

11

When your board makes the rotation, stomp your feet over the bolts and ride away. Now try a heelflip.

Kickflip photo credits
Sequence of Steve Badillo, kickflip gap
Photographer: Gavin Badillo

22

360 Kickflip

360 Kickflip

One of the variations of the kickflip that Mr. Rodney Mullen created was the 360 kickflip, aka tre flip. Sometime after his invention of the kickflip, around 1984, Rodney experimented with the 360 kickflip on his freestyle board, but this was too advanced for most skaters to keep up with. It wasn't until the late '80s and early '90s that the influence of the tre flip was realized.

With pros like Matt Hensley, Jovante Turner and Mike Carroll, the 360 flip became a trick with many different styles, pops and aesthetically pleasing rotations. Many skaters can do them, but some do it so smoothly and with killer board control.

One skater known to stomp tre flips is Jason Lee. For some insane examples of the 360 kickflip, check out Lee's skate parts in the legendary skate flick, *Blind: Video Days.* He shows style with his 360 kickflip to fakie on banks and mini ramps.

The tre flip has become a trick that is compulsory and is common in many video parts for professional skaters. Most skaters learn to do this trick. Because you can do so many variations on such a wide variety of obstacles, the 360 flip will go down as a featured legendary street trick.

> *... staple street trick ... not really the difficulty of the technical aspect of the trick but more about the way someone does the trick.*
> — Richard Mulder

360 kickflip photo credits
Sequence of Nick Mclouth, 360 kickflip gap
Photographer: Steve Badillo

You can do this trick at any speed. Get your feet into the kickflip position. Bend your knees and snap your ollie. As you snap the ollie, flick the board with your front foot to start the backside 360 rotation. Use your

tail foot to help the board spin around. Keep your knees bent and up above the board. Let the board rotate all the way around under your feet. When the board comes around griptape side up, stomp the

landing. Try to land over the bolts. Roll away feeling stoked.

23 Ollie
North

Ollie North
Another of the many tricks Rodney Mullen invented was the one-footed ollie, aka Ollie North. This trick was done during his freestyle period in the early '80s, but became famous again when the street pros did them over fire hydrants in the early '90s. Skaters like Ron Allen, Matt Hensley, Natas and Salman Agah added variations to the one-footed ollie with style in their video roles of the late '80s and early '90s.

When the *Tony Hawk Pro Skater* video game was released, the one-footed ollie was renamed the Ollie North, changing the name of this trick for a whole new generation of skaters. Skaters in the mid-'80s and early '90s called it the one-footed ollie or ollie one foot. The name Ollie North comes from the soldier, Oliver "Ollie" North, who gained notoriety in the late '80s for his involvement in the Iran-Contra affair.

The name Ollie North comes from the soldier, Oliver "Ollie" North who gained notoriety in the late '80s for his involvement in the Iran-Contra affair.

I like this trick because it adds an interesting dimension to the ollie. There is a degree of difficulty with the one-footed version since you leave your board for a split second. It requires a high level of focus.

This trick was taken even further with the variation madollie, which is the one-footed ollie to tail on ramps made famous by Danny Way and Tony Hawk.

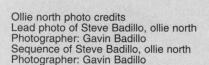

Ollie north photo credits
Lead photo of Steve Badillo, ollie north
Photographer: Gavin Badillo
Sequence of Steve Badillo, ollie north
Photographer: Gavin Badillo

Roll up with any speed depending on the terrain you are riding. You should have your feet in the ollie position. Snap the biggest ollie you can and start to pull your front foot up toward the nose. When you bring your foot up, hit the nose with your front foot so the

board can level out as you kick your foot out. Bring your foot back to the board as you start to land. Try to land on the bolts. Roll away.

9

10

11   12   13

24 Sal Flip

Sal Flip

The sal flip is one of my favorite tricks. I first learned how to do sal flips off launch ramps around 1990. My friend Paul and I were skating a launch ramp outside the skate shop that sponsored us. We had a practice day once a week.

A couple of days earlier I almost landed a sal flip on my launch ramp and wanted to land it in front of my friends. So on our team's skate practice day, I remember Brian Igucci launching tuck knee and Japan airs and my friend Paul doing rocket airs. I warmed up with a frigit air and a judo air. I felt good and everyone was ripping. Finally I went for the sal flip, caught the nose, flipped the board around wide 360, went to land it and landed with my toes on the edge of the board. The board flipped, smacking my shins. I fell forward and slammed. I was bummed because everyone was still sessioning the ramps and my shins were bleeding. Then my friend Paul came over to me and told me something that has stayed with me ever since — It is not how many times you fall but whether you get up and skate. I got back into the lineup and tried the sal flip again. This time I had confidence and landed it. I was stoked. Now I do

different variations like sal flip to disaster, sal flip body variel and sal flip transfers in skateparks.

Sal Barbier invented the sal flip in 1989 skating for H-Street skateboards. His sal flip to fakie on banks was with a nice, smooth, quick style in the H-Street video, *Hokus Pokus*. This trick is legendary because pro skaters are still using it as a unique trick. It's also combined with other tricks to make unusual maneuvers such as a flamingo-sal flip out. The sal flip has directly influenced my skating and is one of my go-to tricks.

Sal flip photo credits
Headshot of Sal Barbier
Photographer: Steve Badillo
Lead photo of Steve Badillo, sal flip to disaster
Photographer: Gavin Badillo
Sequence of Steve Badillo, sal flip to disaster
Photographer: Gavin Badillo

This is a sal flip disaster. Skate up the transition with medium speed or just enough to blast an air. As you almost hit the lip, begin by reaching down with your backside hand and grab the nose turning your fingers to the griptape side. Your thumb should be on

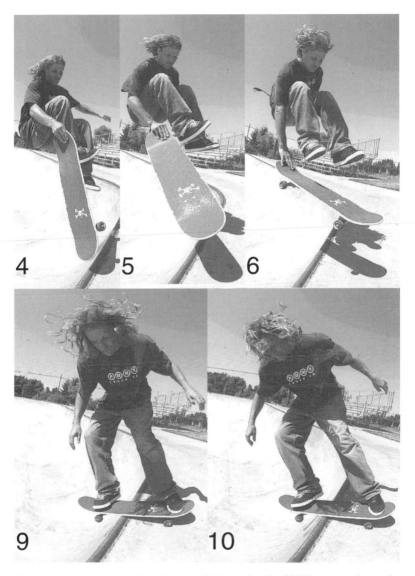

the wood side or bottom of the deck. With your hand start swinging the board wide around 180 degrees underneath you and turn your wrist at the same time. Square up with the bolts as you stomp the disaster.

Lean on your front foot as you roll back into the transition. Don't hang up on the way down by lifting your tail to clear the lip. Compress. Roll away. Try it with your eyes closed.

25 Blunt

> *It's definitely one of my favorite tricks, you can do so many different variations.*
> — Daewon Song

Blunt
The blunt is definitely a legendary trick. It was invented in the streets in the late '80s. It is a unique trick with an abundance of variations for different terrains.

The origin of this trick is a little murky but ultimately starts with two pro skaters of the late '80s. Aaron Deeter, a street pro for Zorlac Skateboards, figured it out on the streets of Seattle and then took it to a vert ramp and pulled it. Some skaters said it would be impossible to do and had to see it to believe it. Aaron's first Zorlac ad shows him doing the blunt on a ramp. But around the same time, a progressive, pure street skater named Tom Knox was also doing blunts on curbs, banks and ramps.

Tom was influential in his skating because he added variations to tricks with speed. In Hawaii at the age of 16, Tom entered his first pro mini ramp contest. During the practice session, Tom did a blunt disaster in front of Tony Hawk. Tony said, "What was that?" Tom told him it was a blunt disaster. Tony had

never seen one before.

I learned how to do the blunt in 1990 skating with my friend Ronnie at his ramp. We were learning blunt variations. He bet me a quarter to see who could land a blunt to pivot fakie first. I won the bet and still have the quarter that he gave me. The blunt pivot to fakie is one of my staple tricks. That is why I still have the quarter.

All through the '90s the blunt increased with popularity, being a trick driven with style and difficulty. Then the blunt was taken to the next level with pros like Daewon Song who is a master blunt skater. He learned the blunt in 1990 but has improved upon the trick ever since. His variations of the blunt are legendary. His combos into and out of the blunt are like he is playing a video game — blunt 360 flip out, kickflip blunt kick-flip out, blunt ollie to late indy grab to fakie and many more variations are weapons in Daewon's arsenal.

This is a frontside bluntslide, a variation of the blunt. Ride toward the coping with medium speed to slide and roll away. Spread your feet out. Hit the coping going frontside and push your tail foot into a blunt while putting your weight on that tail to start the slide.

3

4

7

Twist your shoulders upward a bit so the board can slide. When you get to the end of the ramp, ollie off the coping and swing the nose around frontside with your front foot. Stay on top of the board and skate away.

Blunt photo credits
Lead photo of Steve Badillo, blunt
Photographer: Becca Badillo
Sequence of Steve Badillo, frontside bluntslide
Photographer: Eddie Hadvina

26 K-Grind

K-Grind

A legendary grind heard around the world is the K-grind, named after the great pro skater Eric Koston. The K-grind, aka crooked grind or crook, was actually invented by Dan Peterka in 1990. Dan was skating for H-Street and started doing a combination of the nosegrind and noseslide thus forming a new style of grind.

Eric Koston took the grind and made it famous by adding stylish variations like kickflip out of the grind. He mastered the trick with his natural ability and skaters soon started to call it the K-grind. But Koston is rumored to have called the trick the Peterka grind. Being the modest guy he is, he did not want the trick called the K-grind because he did not invent it.

A legendary grind heard around the world ...

So then it was known as the crooked grind because of the way it looks while doing it. Many street pros use this trick with different variations and on different terrains including rails, ledges, banks and ramps. It's one of the most versatile and recognizable tricks in skateboarding.

I really like the way Salman Agah, Mike Carroll and Henry Sanchez did the K-Grind.
— Chico Brenes

K-grind photo credits
Lead photo of Steve Badillo, k-grind
Photographer: Gavin Badillo
Sequence of Steve Badillo, k-grind
Photographer: Gavin Badillo

Approach the ledge with enough speed at a slight angle to grind the whole ledge. Bend your knees and snap the ollie. As you ollie up and over the top of the ledge, aim the nose down and lock in a nose grind. When the truck locks in, turn the tail out away from

the ledge to be in the crooked position. Put your weight on your front foot and grind to the end of the ledge. To come off, shift your weight back to the tail and level out the board as you land. Stoked.

27 Bigspin

> *Chico Brenes has the best frontside bigspin in the game.*
> — Torey Pudwill

Bigspin
If you have ever bought a scratcher lottery ticket in California, you know what the "Big Spin" game is. Brian Lotti was one of the originators of today's technical street skating. Lotti rose to fame in the late '80s for H-Street skateboards and peaked in popularity in the early '90s for companies like Planet Earth and Blind. Brian's friend Sal Barbier thought his last name "Lotti" sounded like "lottery" and named the trick bigspin. This trick was actually done before Brian Lotti, but his progressive skating and his catchy name helped popularize the bigspin.

Powell Peralta owned a skatepark in Santa Barbara called the Skate Zone where I skated all the time. I learned bigspin transfers at the park's bowl halfpipe spine. Skate Zone had a lot of ramp and street contests and I entered a few of them. In one bowl/ramp

contest, I busted out the bigspin transfer near the end of my run, which put me in third place. I was stoked just to land the bigspin and to have a good run.

I first learned this trick fakie on flat ground. This version of the bigspin is known as the Rick flip after the influential pro skater Rick Howard.

Bigspin photo credits
Lead photo of Steve Badillo, nollie bigspin
Photographer: Gavin Badillo
Sequence of Steve Badillo, nollie bigspin
Photographer: Gavin Badillo

This variation of the bigspin is with a nollie. At any speed ride up the bank with your feet in the nollie position. Curl the toes of your back foot around the inside of the tail to help spin the board. Snap the nollie and spin the board 360 shuvit backside while

3 4

7 8

jumping up in the air bending your knees. Turn your body 180 as the board spins around underneath you. Try to land on the bolts as the board comes around. Lean back into the transition and roll away. Now try it frontside.

Bigspin

9

10

11

12

28 Flamingo

Flamingo
This trick originates with a ripping skater named Dorian Tucker, who developed the trick with his friends and created the template for what became the flamingo. This trick came to life at Mission Bay High School when Dorian was messing around a broken down quarter pipe. He was swinging the board around, catching it behind his leg and then coming back down the ramp. After struggling with it for about an hour, it started to click. Dorian then filmed video footage of it for the Pig Video, *All Systems Go*. Dorian's friends coined different names for the unusual trick like figure 4 and Dorian's favorite, the girl getter. The flamingo is also known as the brain surgeon.

The flamingo was noticed finally by the skateboarding media when Mike Vallely added his own style and variation to it around 2000. Mike learned it in about an hour and thought it wasn't difficult, but the trick looked different from most other tricks. He thought it looked more like a flamingo and called it that when he brought it to the forefront of his skating. Since then, it has become Mike Vallely's signature move with variations like flamingo 180, flamingo to fakie on banks and others.

I remember learning the flamingo hanging out with Adam Alfaro on the set of *Lords of Dogtown*. Waiting to shoot the next scene for the movie, he and I would do flat ground tricks to pass the time. Adam made it look so easy to do, so he showed me how to scoop the board and catch it behind my leg. I learned it in about 20 minutes. Now I do the flamingo when there is a nice bank transition to skate. This trick also gained a lot of fame from *Tony Hawk Pro Skater* with Mike Vallely's character missions.

> *What's great about the flamingo is that young skaters or new skaters are never really ready for it, it kind of catches them off guard. It's not a very traditional looking maneuver, but it's one of my favorites.*
>
> — Mike Vallely

Flamingo photo credits
Sequence of Steve Badillo flamingo
Photographer: Gavin Badillo

> *I always thought it was an eye-catcher of a trick, maybe the best parlor trick of all time.*
> — Dorian Tucker

Try this on flat ground before you do it on a bank. Have your feet in the ollie impossible position with your tail foot griping the edge of the board with your toes and your front foot in the crease of the board with your heel hanging off. Snap an ollie, as the tail

smacks the ground, pull your front foot off and out of the way. Now with your tail foot scoop the board as you ollie. Plant your front foot on the ground and swing the board around the back of that leg with your tail foot.

To land it, use your tail foot to bring the nose of the board around by pulling it forward. Jump up with the planted foot when the board starts turning under you. Set your feet. What about the flamingo nosepick?

29 900

900

Tony Hawk, aka Chairman of the Board, created a wish list of tricks that he wanted to achieve. Throughout his skating career he checked off all the tricks until only one remained — the 900. He first tried to do the 900 in France around 1986, but Hawk could not commit to the spin needed to rotate the full 900. Then in 1997 Tony made that commitment and was able to spin all the way around but came up short on the landing. His injuries were severe enough and the fear was fresh enough to keep him from coming close again for two years. Finally in 1999, with the support of the world at the X-Games, he landed it on live TV, winning the best trick. He was finally able to check off the last trick on his wish list. Of all the tricks Tony Hawk has invented or made famous, the 900 stands alone as the pinnacle of vert tricks. It gave skateboarding

> *The congratulations that meant the most to me were from other skaters. A lot of them called. Danny Way's meant a lot to me, because he was one skater whom I'd been trying the trick with for all those years.*
>
> — Tony Hawk
> Occupation: Pro Skateboarder

a big shot of excitement and inspired other vert pro skaters to take the 900 even further.

Way back in 1989, Danny Way was rumored to have done the 900 in an H-Street video, but he didn't really land it. After Tony Hawk did the 900 at the X-Games, other skaters have attempted it including Tas Pappas and Bob Royce. Then in 2004 Georgio Zattoni and Sandro Dias landed the elusive 900 within a week of each other. Though Tony Hawk has finally landed this holy grail of vert tricks, he has no interest in spinning this trick into the 1080 or more. That will be for some other gnarly vert skater. Though I think it may be some time before anyone achieves it.

Instructions

OK, here goes. Find yourself the biggest ramp you can. Go as fast as you can. I suggest doing back-to-back backside airs and huck yourself trying to spin backside. Have someone watching you and ready to call 911 when you slam.

900 photo credits
Lead photo of Tony Hawk
Photographer: Getty Images

30

Great Wall of
China 360 Air

Great Wall of China 360 Air
In China on July 9, 2005, Danny Way made history. At the historic Juyongguan Gate, the largest and most traveled portion of the Great Wall, Danny skated the world's largest ramp ever constructed. His goal was to be the first person to do an air over the Great Wall of China without the use of a motorized device. A mountain biker died in 2002 attempting the stunt.

Danny met with the Chinese Minister of Extreme Sports for permission to do this sick air. With the go-ahead, Danny was that much closer to his goal. He prepared for a year, training, practicing on the megaramp and even helped design the special ramp for this unique jump. When July came around, Danny was amped. The ramp was in place, cameras ready.

> *Skateboarding has yet to realize its full potential, and by bringing this event to the people of China and the rest of the world, I hope I've contributed to the future of skateboarding and helped bring my sport the global attention it deserves.*
>
> — Danny Way
> Statement from Quicksilver

Unfortunately, in the days leading up to the feat, Danny misjudged and injured his ankle during a practice run. Fearing that the event would be canceled, Danny pushed through his pain and would not leave China before accomplishing his goal. On that Saturday evening, his heart pounding in his chest, Way dropped in the megaramp, cleared the monument and went down. He did not land his trick. He took the long trip back to the top of the enormous structure and tried again. In front of dignitaries, adoring fans and the world, Danny launched over the Great Wall of China and nailed the trick. He went back to the top of the megaramp and landed the 360 air three more times that day.

Danny Way is the personification of perseverance, determination, progression and natural skateboarding talent.

Go as fast as you can to have a good rotation. As you approach the coping, start reaching down with your backside hand to grab the board. Hit the lip with your back wheels and huck yourself into your backside 360 rotation. Turn your head and shoulders

down toward the ground as the rotation starts.
Staying centered, hang on to the board and keep
turning your head. The board will follow you if you
keep your upper body rotating backside.

9

10

11

During the last 90 degrees of turning around let go of the board and straighten out the nose. Land and compress. Skate away.

Great Wall of China 360 air photo credits
Lead photo of Danny Way, backside 360 air
Photographer: Getty Images
Headshot of Danny Way
Photographer: Steve Badillo
Sequence of Tom Schaar, backside 360 air
Photographer: Steve Badillo

31 SkateLab

SkateLab riders
Gavin Badillo
Roy Canright
Finner
Todd Huber
Pixie Iwata
Gage Kamakura
Thelen McKinna-Worrell
Alex Midler
Lance Newton
Mr. Pants
Corey Philips
Michael Randolph
John Schaar
Riley Simone
Snot
Evan Wasser
Jack Ziehl

Photos by Steve Badillo

32 More

Rider: Frank Atwater, Photographer: Steve Badillo

Bibliography

360flip.com. "Tony Hawk." http://www.360flip.com/interviews/tony_hawk.htm, 2007.

Blender, Neil. My Space: Neil Blender. http://profile.myspace.com/
index.cfm?fuseaction=user.viewprofile&friendid=7852136, 2007.

Borte, Jason. Surfline.com, "Larry Bertlemann (August 7, 1955-)." http://www.
surfline.com/surfaz/surfaz.cfm?id=757, 2001.

Burnett, Michael. "Jeff Grosso." Thrasher Magazine, (The Interview Issue), 2007.

Cliver, Sean. *Disposable*. Thornhill, Ontario, Canada: Concrete Wave Productions,
2004.

Concrete Disciples. "Eric Dressen Interviewed."
http://www.concretedisciples.com/cd_articles/eric_dressen/eric_dressen.php, 2007.

Cooper, Lynn. Skatelagends.com, "Profile: Alan Gelfand."
http://www.skatelegends.com/alan_ollie_gelfand.htm, 2007

Craft, Kevin. "15 Things: Hosoi." Skateboarder Magazine, 2007.

Crailtap.com. "Lance Mountain 5."
http://www.crailtap.com/c3/feature_features/fives/fives_lance.html, 2007.

Eisenhour, Mackenzie. "15 Things You Didn't Know About Ed Templeton."
Skateboarder Magazine, 2003.

Floridaskater.com. Kelly Lynn Profile "Florida's First Kelly."
http://www.floridaskater.com/floridaskater%20kelly%20lynn%20profile.htm, 2007.

Haider, Saba. "Tensor Trucks." Transworld Business Magazine, 2001.

Hawk, Tony. *Hawk*. New York, New York: Regan Books, 2001.

Inouye, Tom. My Space: Wally. http://profile.myspace.com/
index.cfm?fuseaction=user.viewprofile&friendID=3574620, 2007.

Juice Magazine. "Tom Knox Interview by Eric Dressen."
http://www.juicemagazine.com/TOMKNOX.html, 2007.

King, Jennifer Carolyn. *Up, Up & A"Way," Way Over The Great Wall of China:
Skateboarder Danny Way Makes History*, Rugged Elegance, 2005.

Lynn, Kelly. "About KL." http://www.kellylynn.com/pages/aboutklset.html, 2007.

Mackaye, Ian. "Duane Peters." Juice Magazine #58, 2007.

Mullen, Rodney. *The Mutt*. New York, New York: Regan Books, 2004.

Newby, Tim. "Rising Son – The Legend of Christian Hosoi." Glide Magazine, 2007.

Peralta, Stacy. Ollieair.com. www.ollieair.com, 1999, 2002.

Scholastic. Ollie, Wally and Bert.
http://teacher.scholastic.com/scholasticnews/indepth/Skateboarding/articles/
index.asp?article=tips&topic=0, 2007.

Scientific American. "Asphalt Acrobats." http://www.sciam.com/specialissues/
0900sports/0900tesler.html, 2001.

Secrets of Success. "The Christian Hosoi Story."
http://www.secretsofsuccess.com/people/hosoi.html, 2007.

Skateamerica.com. "15 Things You Didn't Know About Eric Dressen."
http://www.skateamerica.com/sitemap/content/pages/15-Things-You-Didn-t-Know-
About-Eric-Dressen-3955.html, 2007.

Skateamerica.com. "Eric Koston Bio." http://www.skateamerica.com/sitemap/
content/pages/Eric-Koston-Bio-4360.html, 2007.

Skateboarder Magazine Vol. 5, #6. "Alan Gelfand 15 years old, rides for
Powell/Peralta." Surfer Publications, 1979.

Sportskool. "Mike Vallely – Flamingo & Spinning Handplant Trick Tips."
http://vids.myspace.com/index.cfm?fuseaction=vids.individual&VideoID=4352859,
2007.

Thrasher. *Insane Terrain*. New York, New York: Universe Publishing, 2001.

Thrasher. "Junk Drawer."
http://www2.thrashermagazine.com/junkdrawer/photos/tony_hawk_delmar.html, 2007.

Tonyhawk.com. "Q And A." http://www.tonyhawk.com/qanda_jan_mar_03.cfm, 2007.

Transworld Skateboarding. "Frontside Boneless One with Steve Caballero."
http://www.skateboarding.com/skate/video/0,23430,1539336-1201475,00.html, 2007.

Transworld Skateboarding. Oceanside, California: Transworld Magazine Corporation,
1-2000.

Wikipedia. "360 Flip." http://en.wikipedia.org/wiki/360_flip, 2007.

Wikipedia. "Alan Gelfand." http://en.wikipedia.org/wiki/Alan_Gelfand, 2007.

Wikipedia. "Big Spin." http://en.wikipedia.org/wiki/Big_spin, 2007.

Wikipedia. "Brian Lotti." http://en.wikipedia.org/wiki/Brian_Lotti, 2007.

Wikipedia. "Christian Hosoi." http://en.wikipedia.org/wiki/Christian_Hosoi, 2007.

Wikipedia. "Danny Way." http://en.wikipedia.org/wiki/Danny_Way, 2007.

Wikipedia. "Kickflip." http://en.wikipedia.org/wiki/Kickflip, 2007.

Wikipedia. "Ollie Impossible." http://en.wikipedia.org/wiki/Ollie_Impossible, 2007.

Wikipedia. "Ray Barbee." http://en.wikipedia.org/wiki/Ray_Barbee, 2007.

Wikipedia. "Rodney Mullen." http://en.wikipedia.org/wiki/Rodney_Mullen, 2007.

YouTube. "Blender skateboarding circa 1985."
http://www.youtube.com/watch?v=mvrB7ZVFRpQ, 2007

YouTube. "Skateboarding Christian Hosoi Christ Air."
http://www.youtube.com/watch?v=6p8fXhWBMIU, 2007.

Resources

Here we have a healthy dose of info about skateboarding as it relates to:

Books
Camps
Magazines
Museums
Organizations
Professional skateboarding events
Shops
Skateparks
Skatepark Designers
Videos
Web sites

For a quick fix go to **skateboarding.com** This is an informative (but not the only) portal into the skateboarding galaxy. For face-to-face, find a skateboard shop and talk to skaters.

Books

Books discovered on Amazon.com and Barnesandnoble.com

Baccigaluppi, John. *Declaration of Independents.* San Francisco, California: Chronicle Books, 2001.

Bermudez, Ben. *Skate! The Mongo's Guide to Skateboarding.* New York, New York: Cheapskate Press, 2001.

Borden, Ian. *Skateboarding, Space and the City.* New York, New York: Berg, 2001.

Brooke, Michael. *The Concrete Wave: The History of Skateboarding.* Toronto, Ontario: Warwick Publishing, 1999.

Burke, L.M. *Skateboarding! Surf the Pavement.* New York, New York: Rosen Publishing Group, Inc., 1999.

Cliver, Sean. *Disposable: A History of Skateboarding Art.* Thornhill, Ontario: Concrete Wave Editions 2004.

Davis, James. *Skateboard Roadmap.* England: Carlton Books Limited, 1999.

Gould, Marilyn. *Skateboarding.* Mankato, Minnesota: Capstone Press, 1991.

Gutman, Bill. *Skateboarding: To the Extreme.* New York, New York: Tom Doherty Associates, Inc., 1997.

Hawk, Tony. *Hawk Occupation: Skateboarder.* New York, New York: Regan Books 2001.

Mullen, Rodney. *The Mutt: How to Skateboard and not Kill Yourself.* New York, New York: Regan Books 2004.

Powell, Ben. *Extreme Sports: Skateboarding.* Hauppauge, New York: Barron's Educational Series, Inc., 1999.

Riggins, Edward. *Ramp Plans.* San Francisco, California: High Speed Productions, 2000.

Ryan, Pat. *Extreme Skateboarding.* Mankato, Minnesota: Capstone Press, 1998.

Shoemaker, Joel. *Skateboarding Streetstyle.* Mankato, Minnesota: Capstone Press.

Thrasher. *Insane Terrain.* New York, New York: Universe Publishing, 2001.

Hardwicke, Catherine. *Lords of Dogtown.* Thornhill, Ontario, Canada: Concrete Wave Editions, 2005.

Camps

IPS
School of Skate
P.O. Box 1530
Hood River, Oregon 97031
School_of_skate@sk8ips.com

Lake Owen
HC 60 Box 60
Cable, Wisconsin 54821
715-798-3785

Magdalena Ecke Family YMCA
200 Saxony Road
Encinitas, California 92023-0907
760-942-9622

Mission Valley YMCA
5505 Friars Road
San Diego, California 92110
619-298-3576

SkateLab
Atlantic Beach Skatecamp
16 W. 3rd St.
Atlantic Beach, Florida 32233
904-249-2529
skatelab.com

SkateLab
Steve Badillo Skate Camp
4226 Valley Fair St.
Simi Valley, California 93063
805-578-0040
skatelab.com

Snow Valley
PO Box 2337
Running Springs, California 92382
909-867-2751

Visalia YMCA
Sequoia Lake, CA
211 West Tulare Avenue
Visalia, California 93277
559-627-0700

Woodward Camp
PO Box 93
132 Sports Camp Drive
Woodward, Pennsylvania 16882
814-349-5633

Woodward Lake Owen
46445 Krafts Point Road
Cable, Wisconsin 54821
715-798-3785

Woodward West
28400 Stallion Springs Road
Tehachapi, California 93561
661-882-7900

Young Life Skate Camp
Hope, British Columbia, Canada
604-807-3718

Magazines

Juice
4090 Valley Meadow Road
Encino, California 91436
310-399-5336
www.juicemagazine.com

Thrasher
High Speed Productions
1303 Underwood Avenue
San Francisco, California 94124
415-822-3083
www.thrashermagazine.com

Skateboarder
Surfer Publications
PO Box 1028
Dana Point, California 92629
www.skateboardermag.com

Transworld Skateboarding
353 Airport Road
Oceanside, California 92054
760-722-7777
www.skateboarding.com

Museums

Board Gallery
Newport Beach, California

Huntington Beach International Skate
and Surf Museum
411 Olive St.
Huntington Beach, California
714-960-3483

SkateLab
4226 Valley Fair St.
Simi Valley, California 93063
805-578-0040
www.skatelab.com

Skatopia
34961 Hutton Rd.
Rutland, Ohio 45775
740-742-1110

Organizations

Action Sports Retailer
Organizer of the Action Sports Retailer
Trade Expos.
949-376-8144
asrbiz.com

C.A.S.L. and P.S.L.
California Amateur Skateboard League
Professional Skateboard League
Amateur and professional contest
organizer.
909-883-6176
Fax 909-883-8036

Extreme Downhill International
1666 Garnet Ave. #308
San Diego, California 92109
619-272-3095

International Association of
Skateboard Companies
P.O. Box 37
Santa Barbara, California 93116
805-683-5676
iascsk8@aol.com
skateboardiasc.org

International Network for Flatland
Freestyle Skateboarding
Abbedissavagen 15
746 95 Balsta, Sweden

KC Projects
Canadian amateur contest organizer.
514-806-7838
kc_projects@aol.com
5148067838@fido.ca

National Amateur Skateboard
Championships
Damn Am Series
National amateur contest organizer.
813-621-6793
skateparkoftampa.com
nascseries.com

N.H.S.S.A.
National High School Skateboard
Association
jeffreystern@roadrunner.com
805-990-4209

National Skateboarders Association of
Australia (NSAA)
Amateur and professional contest
organizer.
61-2-9878-3876
skateboard.asn.au

The Next Cup
Southern California amateur contest
organizer.
858-874-4970 Ext. 114 or 129
www.thenextcup.com

Skateboarding Association of America
Amateur contest organizer.
727-523-0875
www.skateboardassn.org

Skatepark Association of the USA
(SPAUSA)
Resource for skatepark planning /
operating.
310-823-9228
www.spausa.org

Southwest Sizzler
Southwestern amateur contest organizer.
918-638-6492

Surf Expo
East Coast trade show.
800-947-SURF
www.surfexpo.com

Supergirl
www.beasupergirl.com

United Skateboarding Association
(USA)
Skate event organizer and action sport
marketing / promotions.
732-432-5400 Ext. 2168 and 2169
www.unitedskate.com

Vans Shoes
Organizer of the Triple Crown skate
events.
562-565-8267
www.vans.com

World Cup Skateboarding
Organizer of some of skating's largest
events.
530-888-0296
Danielle@wcsk8.com
www.wcsk8.com

Zeal Skateboarding Association
Southern California amateur contest
organizer.
909-265-3420
www.zealsk8.com

Professional skateboarding events

All Girl Skate Jam
www.myspace.com
(Search for All Girl Skate Jam)

Gravity Games H2O
Gravitygamesh20.com

Tony Hawk's Boom Boom Huck Jam
www.boomboomhuckjam.com

Mountain Dew Tour
www.astdewtour.com

Vans Triple Crown of Skateboarding
www.vans.com/vans/events

Warped Tour
www.vans.com/vans/events

X Games
Expn.go.com/expn

Shops and companies

Alva Los Angeles
1086 S. Fairfax Avenue
Los Angeles, California 90019
323-954-7295
www.alvaskates.com

IPS Skateboards
IPS Skate & Snow Shop
13 Oak Street
Hood River, Oregon 97031
541-386-6466
www.sk8ips.com
wally@sk8ips.com
skateshop@sk8ips.com

Skateboarding.com

Skateboards.org

SkateLab
4226 Valley Fair St.
Simi Valley, California 93063
805-578-0040
www.skatelab.com

Steadham Skate Ind.
www.stevesteadham.com
myspace.com/stevesteadham
stevesteadham@hotmail.com
ssteadham@gmail.com
702-416-8331

Tailtap
PO Box 1895
Carlsbad, California 92018
www.tailtap.com

Skateparks

Bear Creek Skatepark
625 Highland Drive
Medford, Oregon

Burnside Projects
Underneath the east side of the
Burnside Bridge
Portland, Oregon

Camarillo Skateboard Park
1030 Temple Avenue
Camarillo, California

Chehalem Skate Park
1201 Blaine Street
Newberg, Oregon

Culver City Skateboard Park
Jefferson Blvd. and Duquesne Ave.
Culver City, California

Brian Haney Memorial Skatepark
Main Street and 13th Street
Aumsville, Oregon

Lincoln City Skatepark
NE Reef Street
Lincoln, City, Oregon

Montclair Skatepark
5111 Benito Street
Montclair, California

Oxnard Skateboard Park
3250 South Rose Avenue
Oxnard, California

Pedlow Skate Park
17334 Victory Boulevard
Encino, California

Skateboarding.com

Skateboards.org

SkateLab
4226 Valley Fair St.
Simi Valley, California 93063
805-578-0040
www.skatelab.com

Ken Wormhoudt Skate Park
225 San Lorenzo Boulevard
Santa Cruz, California

Skatepark designers

Airspeed Skateparks LLC
2006 Highway 101 #154
Florence, Oregon 97439
503-791-4674
airspeed@airspeedskateparks.com
www.airspeedskateparks.com

CA Skateparks, Design / Build and
General Contracting
273 North Benson Avenue
Upland, California 91786
562-208-4646
www.skatedesign.com

Dreamland Skateparks, Gridline Inc.
4056 23rd Avenue SW
Seattle, Washington 98106
206-933-7915
www.gridline.com

Freshpark / Radius 8, Inc.
5900 Hollis Street, Suite S
Emeryville, California 94608-2008
800-490-2709
info@freshpark.com
www.freshpark.com

Ramptech
www.ramptech.com

RCMC Custom Cement Skateparks
www.rcmcsk8parks.com

Spectrum Skatepark Creations, Ltd.
M/A 2856 Clifftop Lane
Whistler, B.C.
V0N 1B2 Canada
250-238-0140
design@spectrum-sk8.com
www.spectrum-sk8.com

Team Pain
864 Gazelle Trail
Winter Springs, Florida 32708
407-695-8215
tim@teampain.com
www.teampain.com

John Woodstock Designs
561-743-5963
johnwoodstock@msn.com
www.woodstockskateparks.com

Videos / instructional

411 Video Productions. The First Step.

411 Video Productions. The Next Step.

Hawk, Tony. Tony Hawk's Trick Tips
Volume I: Skateboarding Basics. 900
Films, 2001.

Hawk, Tony. Tony Hawk's Trick Tips
Volume II: Essentials of Street. 900
Films, 2001.

Thrasher Magazine. How to
Skateboard. San Francisco, California:
High Speed Productions, Inc., 1995.

Thrasher Magazine. How to
Skateboard Better. San Francisco,
California: High Speed Productions,
Inc., 1997.

Transworld Skateboarding. Starting
Point. Oceanside, California, 1997.

Transworld Skateboarding. Trick Tips
with Wily Santos. Oceanside,
California, 1998.

Transworld Skateboarding. Starting
Point Number Two. Oceanside,
California, 1999.

Web sites

www.exploratorium.edu/skateboarding
Glossary, scientific explanations and
equipment for skating.

www.interlog.com/~mbrooke/skategee
zer.html
International Longboarder magazine.

www.ncdsa.com
Northern California Downhill
Skateboarding Association.

www.skateboard.com
Chat and messages.

www.skateboarding.com
Every skater's site by Transworld
Skateboarding magazine.

www.skateboards.org
Parks, shops and companies.

www.skatelab.com
One of Los Angeles area's largest
indoor parks and world's largest
skateboard museum.

www.smithgrind.com
Skate news wire.

www.stevebadillo.net
stevebadillo@roadrunner.com

www.switchmagazine.com
Switch Skateboarding Magazine.
www.tailtap.com
Your direct source for hard to find
books and magazines.

www.thrashermagazine.com
A comprehensive site by Thrasher
magazine.

More web sites

360flip.com
alvaskates.com
answers.com
blackplaguewheels.com
blitzdistribution.com
board-crazy.co.uk
concretedisciple.com
crailtap.com
dvsskate.com
dwindle.com
ehow.com
everything2.com
experiencefestival.com
floridaskater.com
forheavenskate.com
furytruckcompany.com
glidemagazine.com
how2skate.com
imdb.com
juicemagazine.com
juicemagazine.com
kellylynn.com
kidzworld.com
mayaskates.com
myspace.com
ollieair.com
podiumdist.com
premise.tv
rainbowskateparks.com
rodneymullen.net
ruggedelegantliving.com
scholastic.com
secretsofsuccess.com
sk8ips.com

sk8kings.com
skateamerica.com
skateboarddirectory.com
skateboarder2.com
skatelab.com
skatelegends.com
skatepunk.net
skateshooters.com
socalskateparks.com
stevesteadham.com
tailtap.com
thinkquest.org
tonyhawk.com
twsbiz.com
wikihow.com
wikipedia.org
youtube.com

Steve's sponsors

Alva Skateboards
1086 S. Fairfax Avenue
Los Angeles, California 90019
323-954-7295
www.alvaskates.com

Black Plague Wheels
www.blackplaguewheels.com

DVS Shoe Company
955 Francisco Street
Torrance, California 90502
www.dvsshoes.com
www.dvsskate.com

Fury Truck Company
1572 Jason Circle
Huntington Beach, California 92649
714-379-0020
www.furytruckcompany.com

SkateLab
4226 Valley Fair St.
Simi Valley, California 93063
805-578-0040
www.skatelab.com

Index

Steve Badillo has co-authored three top selling skateboarding guides including *Skateboarder's Start-Up, Skateboarding: New Levels* and *Skateboarding: Book of Tricks.* He is a pro skater for Alva Skateboards, runs the SkateLab Skate Camp near Los Angeles, and has worked as a stunt double and actor in numerous commercials and films featuring skateboarding including *Lords of Dogtown.* Steve is the head judge for the National High School Skateboard Association, a nation-wide skateboarding program for high schools.